DATE DUE

The Life Cycle of a

Butterfly

by Lisa Trumbauer

Consulting Editor: Gail Saunders-Smith, Ph.D.

Consultant: Ronald L. Rutowski, Professor,
Department of Biology, Arizona State University

Pebble Books

an imprint of Capstone Press
Mankato, Minnesota

Pebble Books are published by Capstone Press
151 Good Counsel Drive, P.O. Box 669, Mankato, Minnesota 56002
http://www.capstone-press.com

1 2 3 4 5 6 07 06 05 04 03 02

Library of Congress Cataloging-in-Publication Data
Trumbauer, Lisa, 1963–
    The life cycle of a butterfly / by Lisa Trumbauer.
    p. cm.—(Life cycles)
    Includes bibliographical references (p. 23) and index.
    Summary: Simple text and photographs present the life cycle of a butterfly.
    ISBN 0-7368-1181-8
    1. Butterflies—Life cycles—Juvenile literature. [1. Butterflies—Life cycles. 2.
Caterpillars.] I. Title. II. Life cycles (Mankato, Minn.)
QL544.2 .T78 2002
595.78'9--dc21   2001004840

Note to Parents and Teachers

The Life Cycles series supports national science standards related to life science. This book describes and illustrates the life cycle of a monarch butterfly. The photographs support early readers in understanding the text. The repetition of words and phrases helps early readers learn new words. This book also introduces early readers to subject-specific vocabulary words, which are defined in the Words to Know section. Early readers may need assistance to read some words and to use the Table of Contents, Words to Know, Read More, Internet Sites, and Index/Word List sections of the book.

Table of Contents

Photographs in this book show the life cycle of a monarch butterfly.

egg

A butterfly begins life
as an egg.

three days

A caterpillar hatches from the egg. The caterpillar eats the eggshell.

caterpillar

8

The caterpillar eats many leaves. The caterpillar grows quickly.

The caterpillar molts.
It sheds its outer skin
to grow.

chrysalis

12

The caterpillar hangs upside down. It molts into a chrysalis.

butterfly

A butterfly comes out of
the shell of the chrysalis
after about two weeks.
Butterflies can live
for nine months.

A male butterfly courts
a female butterfly.
The two butterflies mate.

The female butterfly lays one egg.

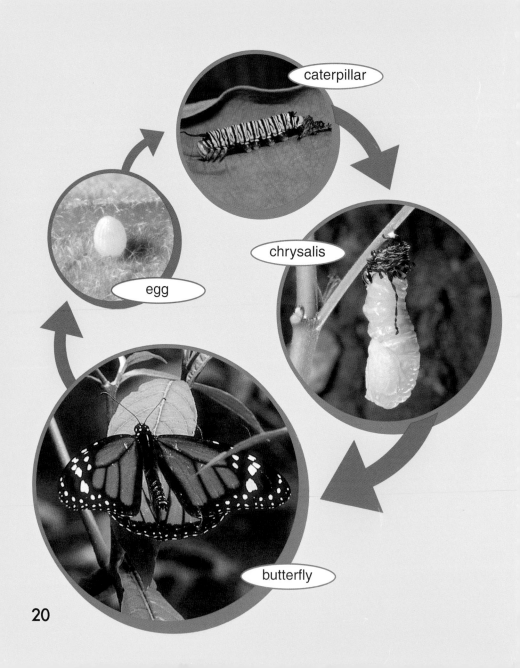

caterpillar

egg

chrysalis

butterfly

The egg is the start
of a new life cycle.

(Words to Know

caterpillar—a worm-like larva that hatches from an egg and molts often; caterpillar is the second life stage of a butterfly.

chrysalis—the third life stage of a butterfly; pupa is another word for chrysalis; a chrysalis has a hard shell.

court—to attract for mating

egg—a small case in which a caterpillar grows; each kind of butterfly lays eggs on a different kind of plant.

hatch—to break out of an eggshell

life cycle—the stages of life of an animal; the life cycle includes being born, growing up, having young, and dying.

mate—to join together to produce young

molt—to shed a skin so that a new skin can grow; caterpillars molt several times as they grow and change form.

shell—a hard covering around an egg or a chrysalis; caterpillars eat their eggshells.

(Read More

Bauman, Amy, and E. Jaediker Nosgaard. *The Wonder of Butterflies.* Animal Wonders. Milwaukee, Wis.: Gareth Stevens, 2000.

Frost, Helen. *Caterpillars.* Butterflies. Mankato, Minn.: Pebble Books, 1999.

Lerner, Carol. *Butterflies in the Garden.* New York: HarperCollins, 2001.

(Internet Sites

All about Butterflies
http://www.enchantedlearning.com/subjects/butterfly

Children's Butterfly Site
http://www.mesc.usgs.gov/butterfly/Butterfly.html

Insecta Inspecta World
http://www.insecta-inspecta.com/butterflies/monarch

(Index/Word List

Word Count: 94
Early-Intervention Level: 13

Editorial Credits

Martha E. H. Rustad, editor; Jennifer Schonborn, production designer and interior illustrator; Kia Bielke, cover designer; Kimberly Danger, Mary Englar, and Jo Miller, photo researchers

Photo Credits

Ann and Rob Simpson, 18

Barrett and MacKay, 16, 20 (bottom)

Dwight R. Kuhn, 10, 20 (top)

Robert & Linda Mitchell, cover (inset)

Unicorn Stock Photos/Ron Holt, cover, 6, 14

Visuals Unlimited/David Cavagnaro, 1; Dick Poe, 4, 20 (left); Bill Beatty, 8; William J. Weber, 12, 20 (right)